Hey, Diddle, Diddle
& other
Nursery Rhymes

Bright ☆ Sparks

This is a Bright Sparks Book
First published in 2000
Bright Sparks
Queen Street House
4 Queen Street
Bath BA1 1HE, UK

This book was created by
The Albion Press Ltd
Spring Hill, Idbury,
Oxfordshire, OX7 6RU, UK

Cover design by
small world creations ltd
Tetbury, GL8 8AA, UK

Printed in China

ISBN 1-84250-122-4

Contents

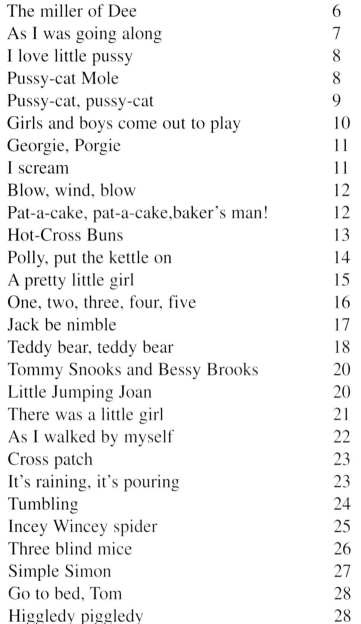

HEY, DIDDLE, DIDDLE

Hey, diddle, diddle, the cat and the fiddle,
The cow jumped over the moon;
The little dog laughed to see such sport,
And the dish ran away with the spoon!

OVER THE HILLS AND FAR AWAY

When I was young and had no sense
I bought a fiddle for eighteenpence,
And the only tune that I could play
Was "Over the Hills and Far Away".

THE MILLER OF DEE

There was a jolly miller
  Lived on the river Dee:
He worked and sung from morn till night,
  No lark so blithe as he;
And this the burden of his song
  For ever used to be—
I jump mejerrime jee!
  I care for nobody—no! not I,
Since nobody cares for me.

AS I WAS GOING ALONG

As I was going along, long, long,
A singing a comical song, song, song,
The lane that I went was so long, long, long,
And the song that I sung was as long, long, long,
And so I went singing along.

I LOVE LITTLE PUSSY

I love little pussy, her coat is so warm;
And if I don't hurt her she'll do me no harm.
So I'll not pull her tail nor drive her away,
But pussy and I very gently will play.

PUSSY-CAT MOLE

Pussy-cat Mole,
Jumped over a coal,
And in her best petticoat burnt a great hole.
Poor pussy's weeping, she'll have no more milk,
Until her best petticoat's mended with silk.

PUSSY-CAT, PUSSY-CAT

Pussy-cat, pussy-cat, where have you been?
I've been to London to see the Queen.
Pussy-cat, pussy-cat, what did you there?
I frightened a little mouse under her chair.

GIRLS AND BOYS COME OUT TO PLAY

Girls and boys, come out to play;
The moon doth shine as bright as day;
Leave your supper, and leave your sleep,
And come with your playfellows into the street.
Come with a whoop, come with a call,
Come with a good will or not at all.
Up the ladder and down the wall,
A halfpenny roll will serve us all.
You find milk, and I'll find flour,
And we'll have a pudding in half-an-hour.

GEORGIE, PORGIE

Georgie, Porgie, pudding and pie,
Kissed the girls and made them cry;
When the boys came out to play
Georgie Porgie ran away.

I SCREAM

I scream, you scream,
We all scream for ice cream!

BLOW, WIND, BLOW!

Blow, wind, blow! and go, mill, go!
That the miller may grind his corn;
    That the baker may take it,
    And into rolls make it,
And send us some hot in the morn.

PAT-A-CAKE, PAT-A-CAKE
BAKER'S MAN!

Pat-a-cake, pat-a-cake, baker's man!
    Bake me a cake, as fast as you can;
Pat it and prick it, and mark it with T,
    And put it aside for Tommy and me.

HOT-CROSS BUNS

Hot-Cross Buns!
Hot-Cross Buns!
One a penny, two a penny,
Hot-Cross Buns!

Hot-Cross Buns!
Hot-Cross Buns!
If you have no daughters
Give them to your sons.

POLLY, PUT THE KETTLE ON

Polly, put the kettle on,
Polly, put the kettle on,
Polly, put the kettle on,
   And we'll all have tea.

Sukey, take it off again,
Sukey, take it off again,
Sukey, take it off again,
   They're all gone away.

A PRETTY LITTLE GIRL

A pretty little girl in a round-eared cap
I met in the streets the other day;
   She gave me such a thump,
   That my heart it went bump;
I thought I should have fainted away!
I thought I should have fainted away!

ONE, TWO, THREE, FOUR, FIVE

One, two, three, four, five,
  I caught a fish alive;
Six, seven, eight, nine, ten,
  I let him go again.
Why did you let him go?
  Because he bit my finger so.

16

JACK BE NIMBLE

Jack be nimble,
And Jack be quick:
And Jack jump over
The candlestick.

TEDDY BEAR, TEDDY BEAR

Teddy bear, teddy bear,
Turn around.
Teddy bear, teddy bear,
Touch the ground.
Teddy bear, teddy bear,
Show your shoe.
Teddy bear, teddy bear,
That will do.

Teddy bear, teddy bear,
Go upstairs.
Teddy bear, teddy bear,
Say your prayers.
Teddy bear, teddy bear,
Turn out the light.
Teddy bear, teddy bear,
Say good night.

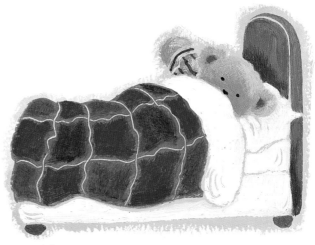

TOMMY SNOOKS AND BESSY BROOKS

As Tommy Snooks and Bessy Brooks
Were walking out one Sunday,
Says Tommy Snooks to Bessy Brooks,
"Tomorrow will be Monday."

LITTLE JUMPING JOAN

Here am I, little jumping Joan.
When nobody's with me,
I'm always alone.

THERE WAS A LITTLE GIRL

There was a little girl, and she had a little curl
Right in the middle of her forehead;
When she was good she was very, very good,
But when she was bad she was horrid.

AS I WALKED BY MYSELF

As I walked by myself,
And talked to myself,
  Myself said unto me,
Look.to thyself,
Take care of thyself,
  For nobody cares for thee.

I answered myself,
And said to myself,
  In the self-same repartee,
Look to thyself,
Or not look to thyself,
  The self-same thing will be.

CROSS PATCH

Cross patch,
  Draw the latch,
Sit by the fire and spin;
  Take a cup,
  And drink it up,
Then call your neighbours in.

IT'S RAINING, IT'S POURING

It's raining, it's pouring,
The old man is snoring;
He went to bed and bumped his head
And couldn't get up in the morning.

TUMBLING

In jumping and tumbling
We spend the whole day,
Till night by arriving
Has finished our play.

What then? One and all,
There's no more to be said,
As we tumbled all day,
So we tumble to bed.

INCEY WINCEY SPIDER

Incey Wincey spider
  Climbing up the spout;
Down came the rain
  And washed the spider out:
Out came the sunshine
  And dried up all the rain;
Incey Wincey spider
  Climbing up again.

THREE BLIND MICE

Three blind mice, see how they run!
Three blind mice, see how they run!
They all ran after the farmer's wife,
Who cut off their tails with a carving-knife,
Did ever you hear such a thing in your life,
As three blind mice.

SIMPLE SIMON

Simple Simon met a pieman
  Going to the fair;
Said Simple Simon to the pieman,
  "Let me taste your ware."

Said the pieman to Simple Simon,
  "Show me first your penny";
Said Simple Simon to the pieman,
  "Indeed I have not any."

GO TO BED, TOM

Go to bed, Tom,
Go to bed, Tom,
Tired or not, Tom,
Go to bed, Tom.

HIGGLEDY PIGGLEDY

Higgledy piggledy,
Here we lie,
Picked and plucked,
And put in a pie!

MONDAY'S CHILD IS FAIR OF FACE

Monday's child is fair of face,
Tuesday's child is full of grace,
Wednesday's child is full of woe,
Thursday's child has far to go,
Friday's child is loving and giving,
Saturday's child works hard for his living,
And the child that is born on the Sabbath day
Is bonny and blithe, and good and gay.

THERE WAS A CROOKED MAN

There was a crooked man, and he went a
   crooked mile,
He found a crooked sixpence against a
   crooked stile;
He bought a crooked cat, which caught a
   crooked mouse,
And they all lived together in a little crooked house.

COME TO BED, SAYS
SLEEPY-HEAD

Come to bed,
Says Sleepy-head;
  "Tarry a while," says Slow;
"Put on the pot,"
Says Greedy-gut,
  "Let's sup before we go."

I SEE THE MOON

I see the moon,
   And the moon sees me;
God bless the moon,
   And God bless me.